My OUTDOOR ACTIVITY DOODLE Book

Amanda Li

Illustrated by Dan Newman

MACMILLAN CHILDREN'S BOOKS

First published 2012 by Macmillan Children's Books
a division of Macmillan Publishers Limited
20 New Wharf Road, London N1 9RR
Basingstoke and Oxford
Associated companies throughout the world
www.panmacmillan.com

ISBN 978-1-4472-1634-6

Text and illustrations copyright © Macmillan Children's Books 2012
Brands and trademarks copyright © The Scout Association 2012
Written by Amanda Li
Design and artwork by Dan Newman
All rights reserved. Gilwell Park, Chingford, London E4 7QW
Registered Charity Numbers 306101 (England and Wales) and
SC038437 (Scotland). Incorporated by Royal Charter.

1 3 5 7 9 8 6 4 2

A CIP catalogue record for this book is available from
the British Library.

Printed and bound by CPI Group (UK) Ltd, Croydon CR0 4YY

www.scouts.org.uk/join

My Outdoor Adventure

by

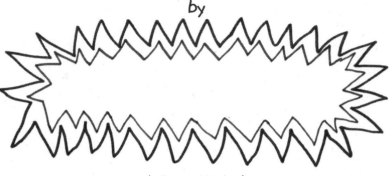

(write your name here)

I am in . . . .
(write name of place)

I arrived on . . . .
(write date)

at . . . .
(write time)

(draw the time)

Who are you with?

Tick the boxes.

- [ ] Beaver Scouts
- [ ] Cub Scouts
- [ ] Mum
- [ ] Dad
- [ ] Brother(s)
- [ ] Sister(s)
- [ ] Friend(s)
- [ ] Dog
- [ ] Other family members
- [ ] School
- [ ] Other . . . .

How long are you staying?

. . . .

HOW DID YOU GET HERE?

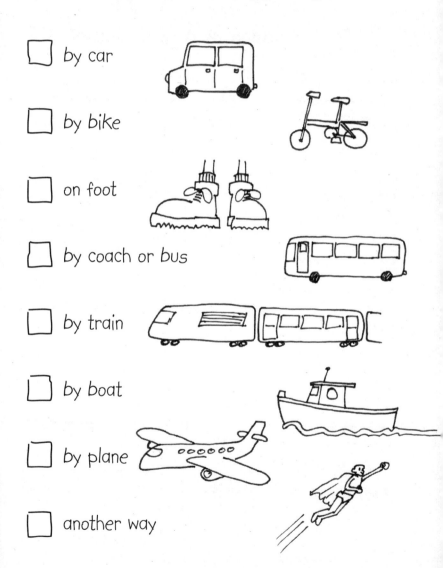

☐ by car

☐ by bike

☐ on foot

☐ by coach or bus

☐ by train

☐ by boat

☐ by plane

☐ another way

Make a sign for your day out

Can you think of a good name?

DRAW A MAP

showing where you are:

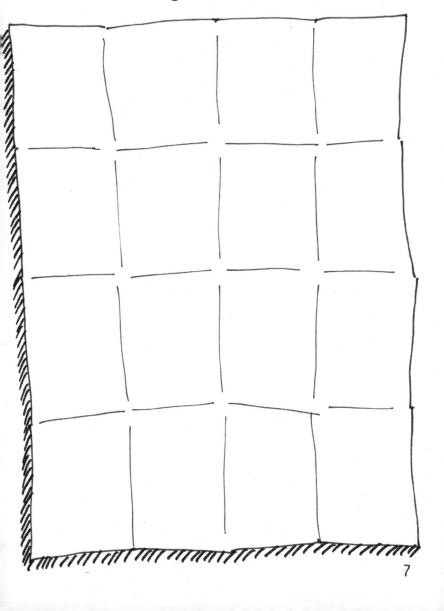

My Compass

Look at the compass. Can you write North, South, East and West?

Remember: Never Eat Soggy Waffles!

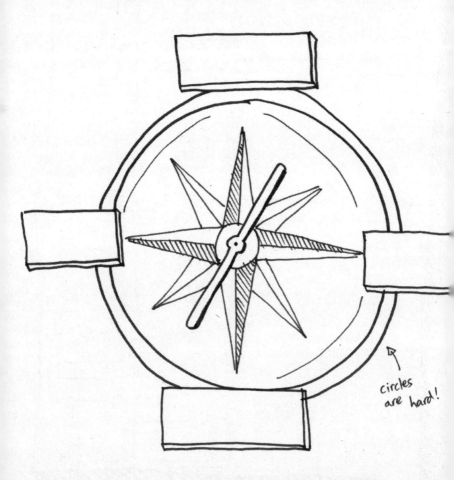

circles are hard!

Where are you sleeping tonight?

in a . . .

☐ tent

☐ caravan or mobile home

☐ hotel

☐ hut

☐ church hall

☐ garden

☐ camper van

☐ somewhere else

. . . .

Draw yourself in the sleeping bag.
Colour and decorate the bag.

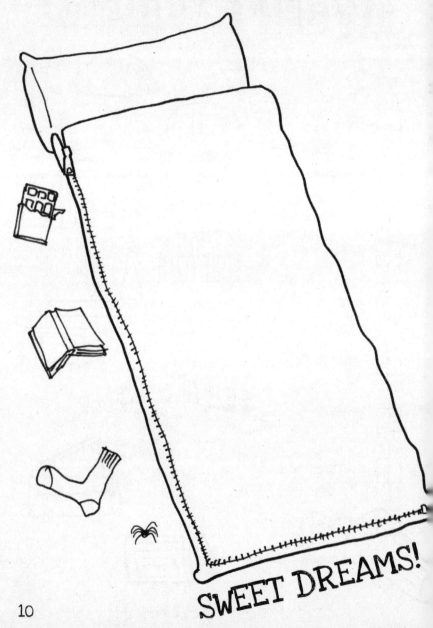

SWEET DREAMS!

THINGS TO DO WHEN IT'S DARK

Look up at the night sky through binoculars or a telescope. What can you see?

☆ Use a torch to make shadow puppets in your tent.

Shine your torch outside. What can you see? Draw it.

where will you go on your outdoor adventure?

Tick the places you'd like to visit.

Beach

Farm

River

Castle

Caves

Woods

Mountain

Park

Other

Your turn

13

WHICH OF THESE THINGS WOULD YOU LIKE TO DO?

Colour or circle your answer.

Go on a treasure hunt
YES NO

Have a picnic

Play games
YES NO

Sleep in a tent
YES NO

Build a den
YES NO

Make a sandcastle
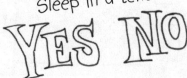

Sing a song
YES NO

What's your dream activity?

Climb a tree
yes no

Take photographs
yes no

Go for a swim
YES NO

Make a campfire
YES NO

Go cycling
YES NO

15

Are you staying in a tent?

Which type?

☐ classic tent

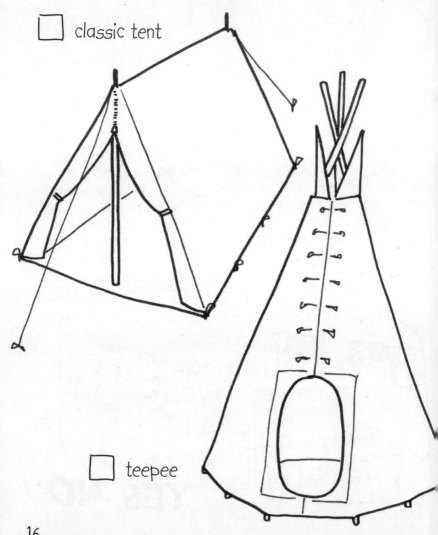

☐ teepee

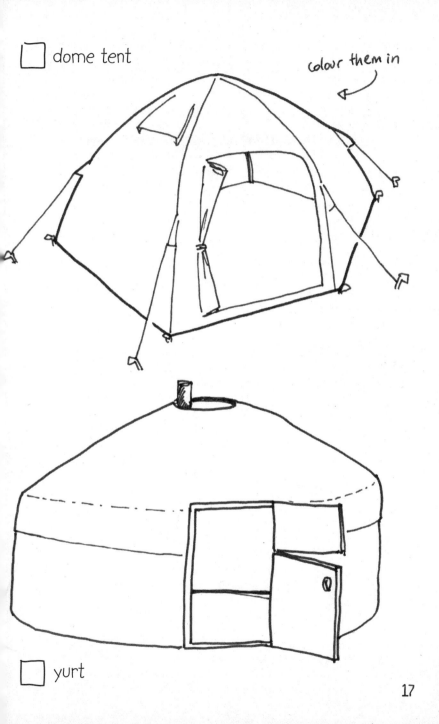

☐ dome tent

colour them in

☐ yurt

MY EQUIPMENT LIST

Draw or write down all the useful
things you've brought with you.

Which thing would you
be the most sad to lose?

. . . .

Which of your things
do you think will be
the most useful?

. . . .

My Equipment

MY RUCKSACK

Design yourself a fantastic rucksack.

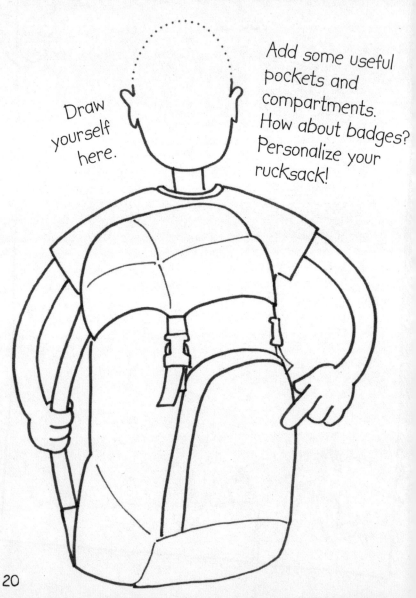

Draw yourself here.

Add some useful pockets and compartments. How about badges? Personalize your rucksack!

Get Spotting!

Tick the boxes of the things you see or find.

☐ **Pine cone**
Look on the ground close to trees.

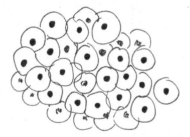

☐ **Frogspawn**
Peer at ponds during springtime.

☐ **Wasp**
Buzz off!

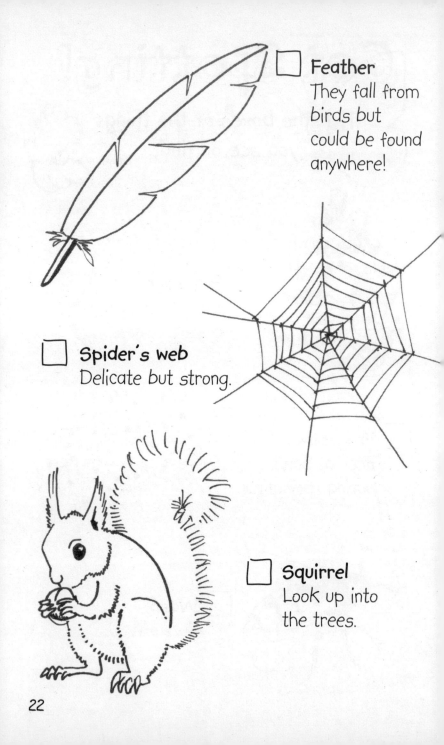

☐ **Feather**
They fall from birds but could be found anywhere!

☐ **Spider's web**
Delicate but strong.

☐ **Squirrel**
Look up into the trees.

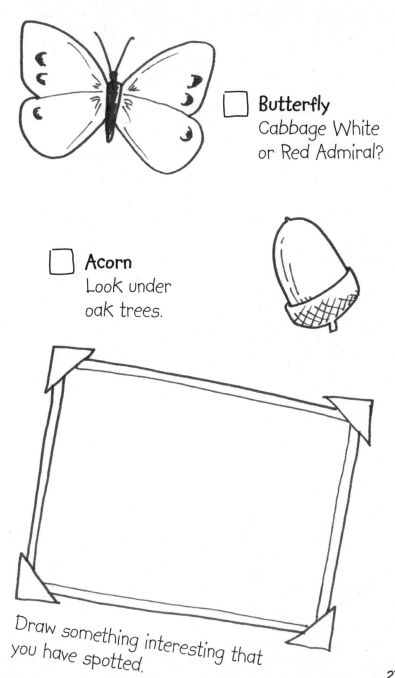

Butterfly
Cabbage White
or Red Admiral?

Acorn
Look under
oak trees.

Draw something interesting that
you have spotted.

23

SKETCH A PLANT

Take a good look
at what's growing around you.

Are there trees, plants and flowers?
Choose an interesting one and look at it
carefully before you draw it. Think about:

 The shape of the leaves or petals.

 Are the edges jagged or smooth?

 What colour is it?

 Is it prickly or hairy?

 How many petals or leaf parts
does it have?

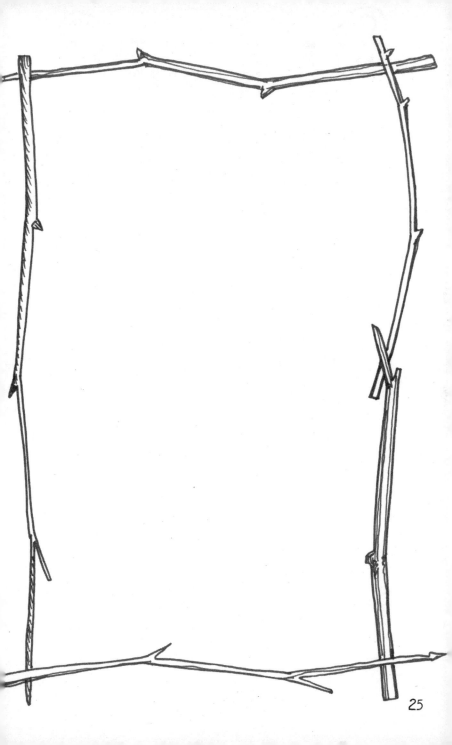

Listen!

Stand quietly and listen to the noises around you. What can you hear? Tick the boxes.

☐ Birds singing

☐ Music

☐ The wind in the trees

☐ Cars driving past

☐ People talking

☐ Planes flying overhead

☐ Water splashing or running

Anything else? Draw it!

Can you smell anything?

Describe it.

. . . .

. . . .

Now close your eyes and hold your hand out. What's the first thing you touch? How does it feel? Circle the word.

ROUGH

smooth

WET

DRY

HARD

SHARP

SQUIDGY

SOFT

Other words . . . .

Get dirty!

Being outdoors means sometimes getting a bit messy.

Draw yourself having a mud bath or getting absolutely soaked!

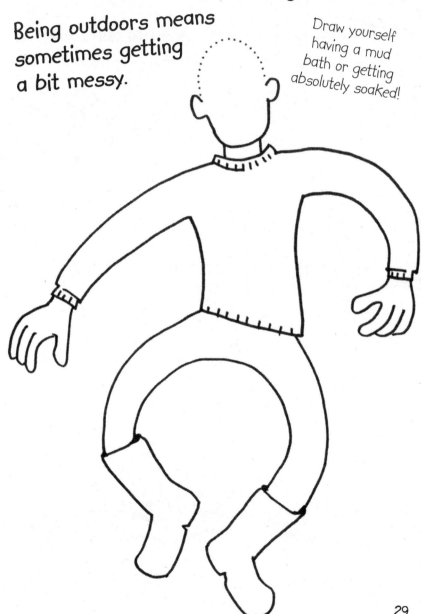

29

Leave a leaf

Take a look at the trees around you.
Can you see any of these leaves?

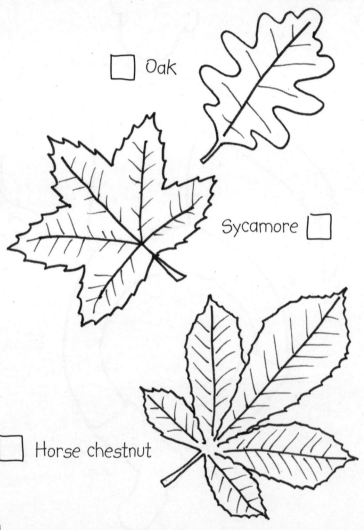

☐ Oak

Sycamore ☐

☐ Horse chestnut

Find a leaf you like and draw it.
Or use a crayon to make a leaf rubbing.

Which tree does your leaf come from?

Did you know? A yew tree can live for 2,000 years.

Did you know? You can tell the age of a tree by counting the rings on the inside of its trunk.

What can you see in a tree?

Write or draw about anything you've seen on a tree

Watch for things falling from trees – like 'helicopters' from sycamore trees.

Look for buds in springtime, seeds like conkers in the autumn.

Look on and under leaves. Can you see any insect eggs? Are there any holes in the leaves where caterpillars have munched their way through?

Stripped bark means squirrels have been around.

Bark makes a good hidey-hole for minibeasts.

Are there any plants growing in the shade?

The roots of a tree can grow far underground.

Look for fallen fruit, nuts and leaves.

What's in the tree?

Add lots of leaves
to the branches.
How about a
bird's nest?

Draw animals in the tree,
like birds and squirrels.

Things to do in the woods (or park or garden)

Make a den
Find a good spot under a tree or in the bushes. Use fallen branches and twigs to build your den.

Go on a bug hunt

Get a bug jar and a magnifying glass and see what you can find! Always gently put the bugs back where they belong.

Make a piece of art
Use stones, twigs, pine cones, leaves and acorns to make a sculpture or a picture.

Press a flower

Collect fallen flowers and press them between newspaper and two heavy books for a week or so. Then glue them into a scrapbook or make a birthday card.

Make a daisy chain

Thread daisies together by making tiny holes through the stalks with your fingernail. If you can't find daisies, try dandelions.

Which is your favourite thing to do? Why?

. . . .

. . . .

. . . .

. . . .

Look under a log

Can you *see* a large stone or a log nearby? Look under and around it. What can you *see*? Tick the boxes.

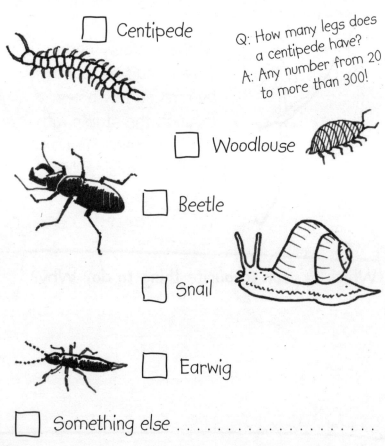

☐ Centipede

Q: How many legs does a centipede have?
A: Any number from 20 to more than 300!

☐ Woodlouse

☐ Beetle

☐ Snail

☐ Earwig

☐ Something else . . . .

Draw what you've found under the magnifying glass.

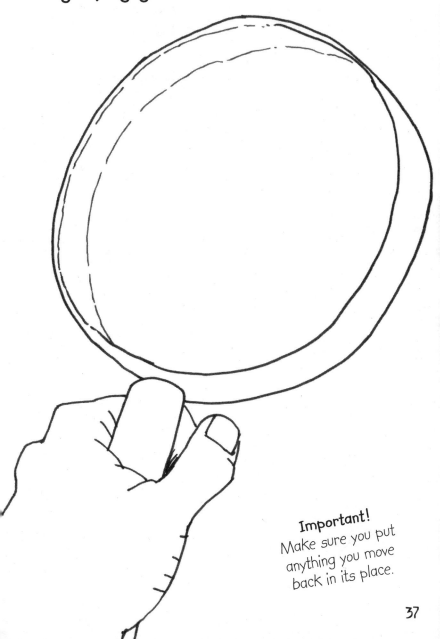

Important!
Make sure you put anything you move back in its place.

MINIBEASTS

Add legs, wings or antennae to the minibeasts' bodies.

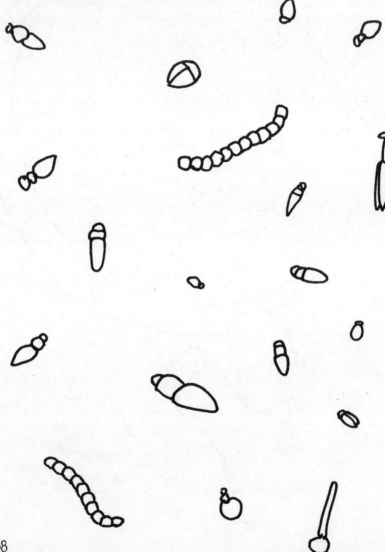

Have you seen any webs nearby?
Draw a spider in the web.

Spiders' webs are very light, but incredibly strong. The spider has special glands which produce silk to make the threads of the web.

What's cooking?

Draw your favourite food to eat outdoors. Mmm, tasty!

'Al fresco' means eating outside – food just seems to taste better that way!

Create your perfect outdoor menu.

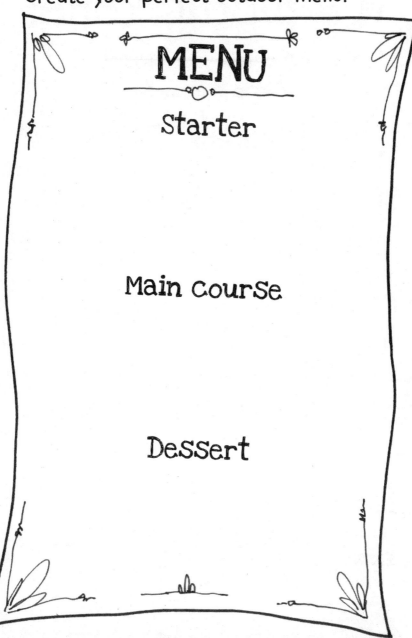

MENU

Starter

Main course

Dessert

It's picnic time!

What's in your picnic?
Circle the words.

sandwiches

rolls

oranges

sausages

apples

pie

crisps

strawberries

carrot sticks

dips

and . . . .

What are you drinking?

Do you have some fruit? Draw it here.

What's inside your sandwich?

What's the best part of your picnic? Write or draw it here.

Tick here when you've picked up all your rubbish afterwards!

What's the weather like?

Draw pictures for each type of weather.

sunny

cloudy

windy

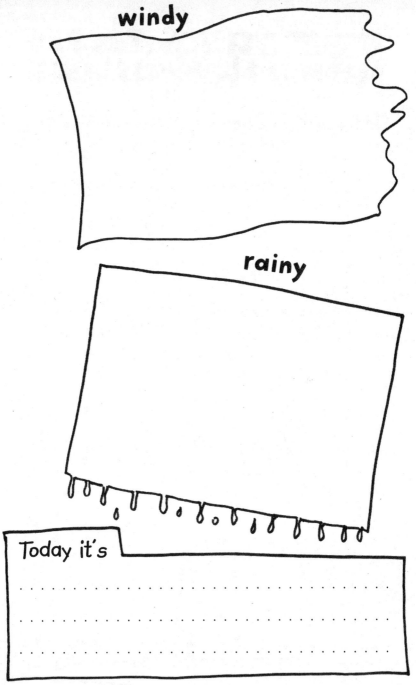

rainy

Today it's

. . . .

. . . .

. . . .

RAINBOW!

Have you seen a rainbow on this trip?
Colour this one in.

To see a rainbow,
you need the sun
behind you and rain
in front of you.

Tip: Indigo is a dark blue.
Violet is a bright purple.

RED

ORANGE

YELLOW

GREEN

BLUE

INDIGO

VIOLET

How to remember the
colours of the rainbow –
'**R**ichard **O**f **Y**ork **G**ave
Battle **I**n **V**ain.'

Get Spotting!

Tick the boxes of the things you see or find.

☐ **Sycamore seed**
Also known as a 'helicopter'.

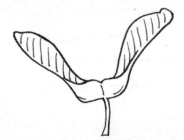

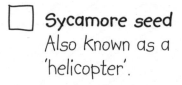

☐ **Dragonfly**
Find them hovering near water.

☐ **Fern**
Look on woodland floors.

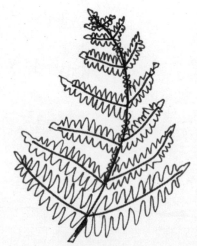

☐ **Duck**
Find on ponds,
streams and
rivers.

☐ **Conker**
Peel off the spiny
green case.

☐ **Shell**
Can you hear
the sea?

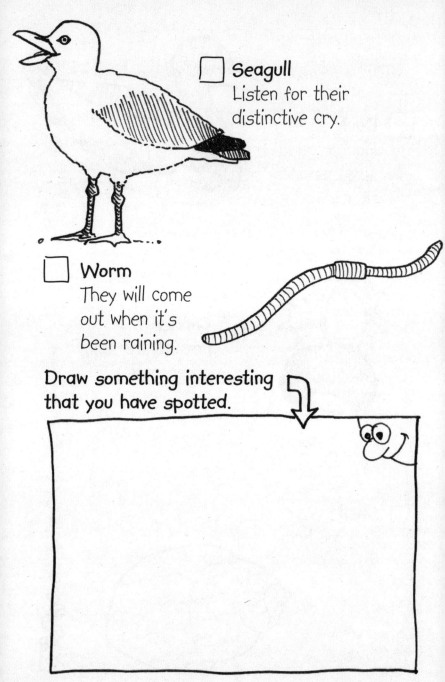

☐ **Seagull**
Listen for their distinctive cry.

☐ **Worm**
They will come out when it's been raining.

Draw something interesting that you have spotted.

THE SEASONS

Draw a picture for each season.

Spring

Summer

Autumn

Winter

What's your favourite season?

. . . .

Why?

. . . .

. . . .

. . . .

What's the weather like in this season?

. . . .

. . . .

. . . .

Are there any special days or
celebrations which happen in this season?

. . . .

. . . .

. . . .

. . . .

. . . .

. . . .

Rainy rhymes

Fill in the missing words.

Rain, rain, go away,
Come again another . . .

Finish this rainy picture. What's getting wet?

Draw some splashy puddles for these boots.

It's raining, it's pouring
The old man is snoring.
He went to bed
And bumped his head
And couldn't get up in the . . . .

I hear thunder, I hear thunder,
Hark, don't you? Hark, don't you?
Pitter patter raindrops
Pitter patter raindrops
I'm . . . through,
So are you!

Draw some lightning from these clouds.

Things to do on a beach

Make a seaside face

Arrange shells, pebbles and seaweed on the sand to make a funny face.

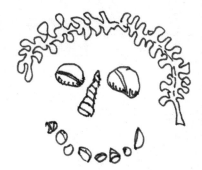

Build a sandcastle

You need a bucket, a spade and plenty of damp sand. Decorate your castle with shells and pebbles.

Write your name

Find a stick or a pebble and write your name
HUGE in the sand!

Explore a rockpool

Look for crabs, shrimps, starfish
and small fish. Use your net gently
and put anything you find back.

Skim a stone

Practise throwing it across the water to make it skim over the surface. Flat, smooth pebbles work best.

Curl your forefinger round the edge of the stone so it spins as you throw it.

Jump the tide!

As the tide comes in, get as near to the water as possible without letting it touch your toes. Get ready to dash back!

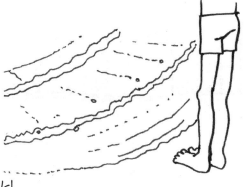

Which is your favourite thing? Why?

. . . .

. . . .

. . . .

. . . .

. . . .

61

on the beach

Finish this picture.

Paint your beach hut

Build a
sandcastle

Draw fish and other creatures
swimming in the sea

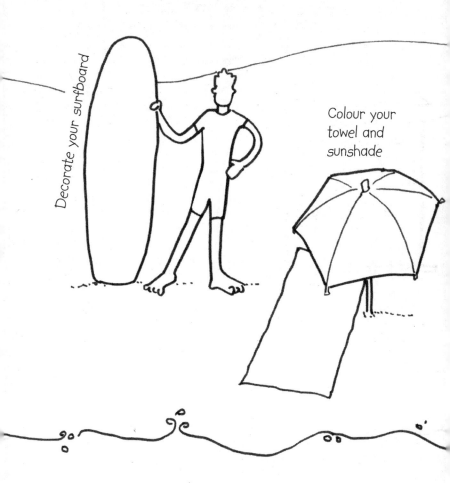

Decorate your surfboard

Colour your towel and sunshade

63

Send a 'postcard' to a friend

welcome to...

Draw or colour a scene – or lots of little pictures – to show your outdoor adventure

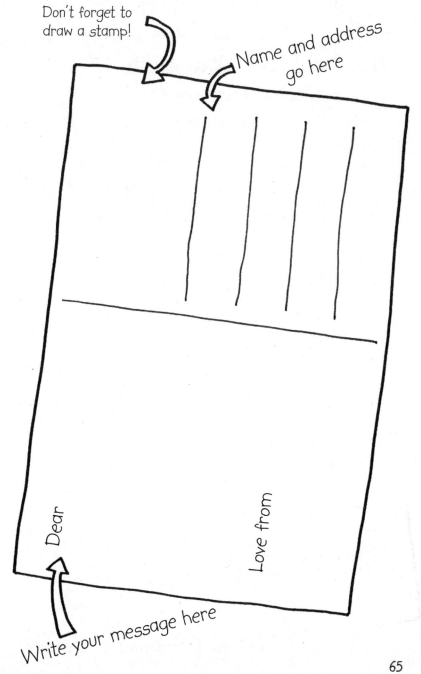

Don't forget to draw a stamp!

Name and address go here

Dear

Love from

Write your message here

BIRDSPOTTING

This Cub Scout is birdspotting.
What can he see?

Draw a bird on the branch.

Are you a good birdspotter?
Write the names of the six birds
beside the pictures.

(bluish-black with a black beak, gathers in groups)

1. ☐ _____

(black and white)

2. ☐ _____

(small, pale brown with a red front)

3. ☐ _____

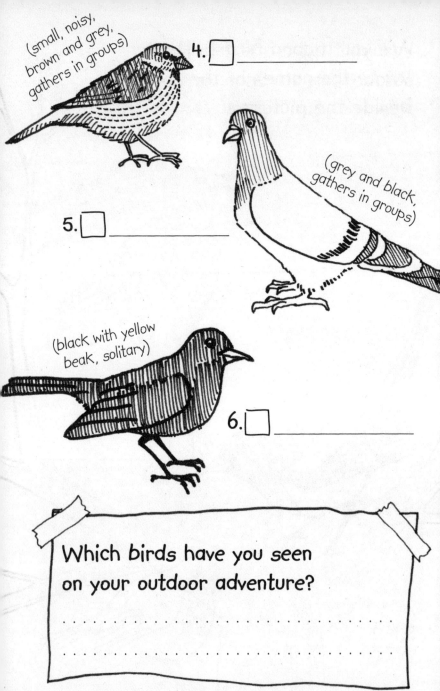

(small, noisy, brown and grey, gathers in groups)

4. ☐ _____

(grey and black, gathers in groups)

5. ☐ _____

(black with yellow beak, solitary)

6. ☐ _____

Which birds have you seen on your outdoor adventure?

. . . .

. . . .

Answers 1. Crow. 2. Magpie. 3. Robin. 4. Finch. 5. Pigeon. 6. Blackbird.

Wouldn't it be great to live outdoors in a treehouse?

Build yourself a dream treehouse – don't forget a ladder!

FUN AND GAMES

Being outdoors means you can run around and play lots of games.

Shadow Tag
'Tag' someone by stepping on his/her shadow.

Spiders and Flies
It's 'tag' – but if you are caught by the 'spider' you must hold hands and try to catch more 'flies'.

Capture the Flag
Try to get the other team's 'flag' – but if you get caught, you have to join their team!

What's the Time, Mr Wolf?
One person is the wolf. Everyone else faces them and chants, 'What's the time, Mr Wolf?' The wolf says, 'One o'clock,' and everyone takes one step forward. (Then two steps for two o'clock, etc.) But when the wolf says, 'Dinner Time!' everyone turns and runs from the wolf. The first to be caught is the next to be wolf!

DINNER TIME!

What's your favourite game?
How do you play it?

. . . .

. . . .

. . . .

. . . .

Let's go on a Scavenger Hunt!

First one back to base with FIVE items from the list below wins the game!

- [ ] Something that has fallen from a tree
- [ ] A smooth stone or pebble
- [ ] A stick
- [ ] A petal
- [ ] Something that has been nibbled by an animal or insect
- [ ] Something green
- [ ] A nut, seed or cone
- [ ] A feather
- [ ] A piece of bark

Who will be the SUPER SCAVENGER?

BZZZ!

Have you seen any **bees** or **wasps** on your outdoor adventure?

Draw lots of bees and make a swarm.

Write three things you know about bees.

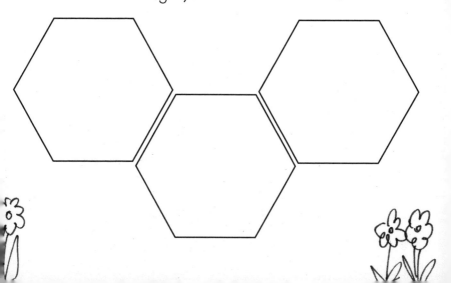

HAVE YOU SEEN ANY ANIMALS ON YOUR ADVENTURE?

☐ Any birds?

☐ Any mammals?

☐ Any amphibians?

☐ Any minibeasts?

☐ Any reptiles?

Draw an animal you've seen –
or one you would like to see . . .

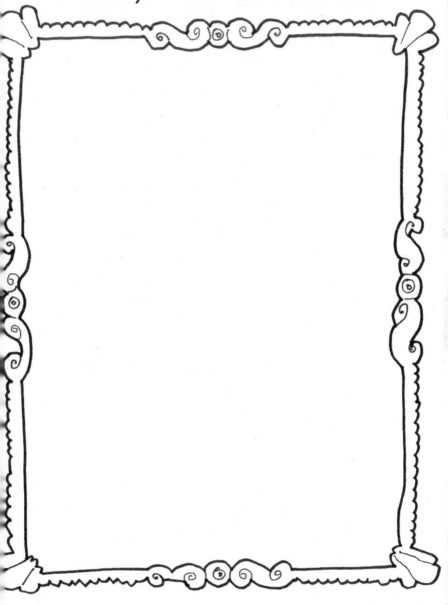

Make Tracks

Have you seen any animal tracks on your adventure? Try matching these tracks with the right animal.

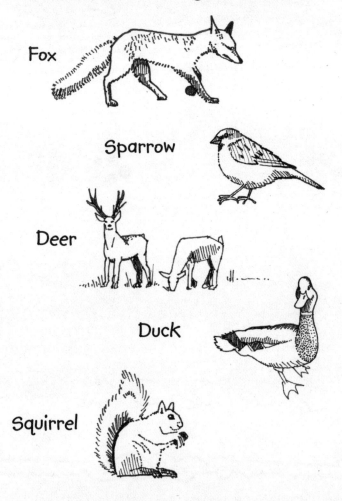

Fox

Sparrow

Deer

Duck

Squirrel

1.

2.

3.

4.

5.

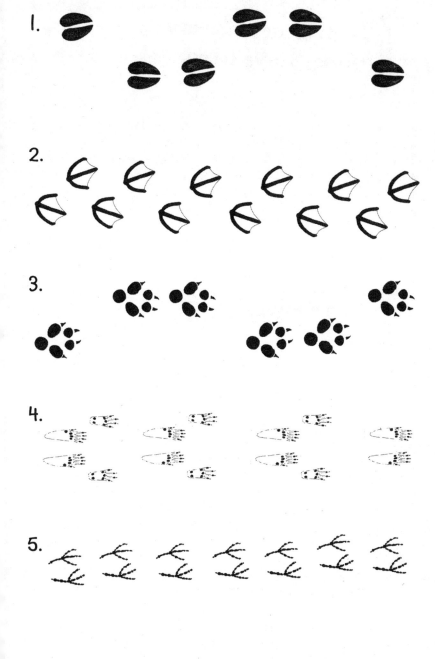

Answers 1. Deer 2. Duck 3. Fox 4. Squirrel 5. Sparrow.

Draw or describe any tracks you've found.

What kind of tracks do you think you would leave?
Draw your tracks — with or without shoes!

Get Spotting!

Tick the boxes of the things you see or find.

☐ **Log**
A paradise for all kinds of minibeasts.

☐ **Woodlice**
They like dark, damp places, especially logs!

☐ **Stinging nettle**
Ouch! Rub any stings with a dock leaf.

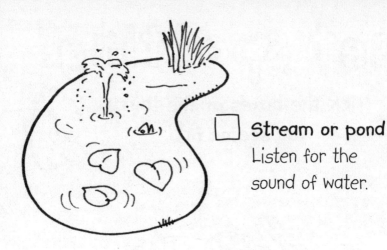

Stream or pond
Listen for the
sound of water.

Ladybird
Look for the
distinctive red
with black spots.

Fish
Rock pools and
streams are
ideal places.

☐ **Caterpillar**
Watch out for
holes in leaves.

☐ **Seaweed**
Gets washed
up on the shore.
Can be a bit
stinky!

Draw something interesting
that you have spotted.

AFTER YOUR TRIP...

Which of these things did you
do on your outdoor adventure?
Tick the boxes.

☐ Cooked a meal on a campfire

☐ Got wet

☐ Played games

☐ Built a den

☐ Told a story

once upon a time...

☐ Wore wellies

☐ Used a compass

☐ Climbed a tree

☐ Got lost

☐ Slept in a tent

☐ Carried a rucksack

☐ Navigated with a map

☐ Tidied/cleaned up

☐ Got muddy

☐ Had a brilliant time!

☐ Anything else?

. . . .

. . . .

. . . .

Circle the words that describe your outdoor adventure. Then add a word of your own.

DANGEROUS

INTERESTING

SCARY SUNNY

TOO LONG

FUN BUSY!!

BEAUTIFUL

HILARIOUS

WARM

84

adventure was . . .

FREEZING

WET

TIRING

AWESOME

BORING

COMPLICATED

UNBELIEVABLE

MEMORABLE

OVER TOO SOON!

THRILLING

Who did you play with
on your outdoor adventure?

. . . .

. . . .

. . . .

Did you meet anyone new? Who?

. . . .

. . . .

Write the names of all the people
(and pets) who went on your outdoor
adventure.

Grown-ups   Children

. . . .

. . . .

. . . .

. . . .

. . . .

. . . .

. . . .

Now draw:

The person who made
you laugh the most

The person who got the
dirtiest or wettest

Pets

. . . .

. . . .

. . . .

. . . .

. . . .

. . . .

. . . .

. . . .

The most sensible
person

MY OUTDOOR ADVENTURE

Draw a funny comic strip about your trip. Let your imagination run wild!

You can use:

How about some sound effects?

ONE DAY...

THE END

Memories

What will you remember about your outdoor adventure? Draw and describe . . .

the best thing you saw . . .

the funniest thing that happened . . .

the weirdest thing you saw . . .

and the most annoying thing that happened!

True or False?

Are these fascinating nature facts true or false? Tick the boxes, then check your answers.

TRUE FALSE

1. A spider is an insect.

2. The Moon travels around the Earth.

3. Conkers come from oak trees.

4. The Atlantic Ocean is the largest ocean on the Earth.

5. Birds have hollow bones, which help them fly.

6. Some trees can live for thousands of years.

7. The Sun rises in the West and sets in the East.

And finally (watch out for this one):

8. Food tastes better when eaten outside.

Answers 1. False. A spider has eight legs and is an arachnid. Insects have six legs. **2.** True. The Moon orbits the Earth, taking about 27 days to complete the cycle. **3.** False. Conkers come from horse-chestnut trees. **4.** False. The Pacific Ocean is the largest. The Atlantic is second largest. **5.** True. **6.** True. **7.** False. The Sun rises in the East and sets in the West. **8.** There's no right answer – it's up to you!

MY PHOTO ALBUM

Did you take any interesting photos
during your adventure? Stick them here.

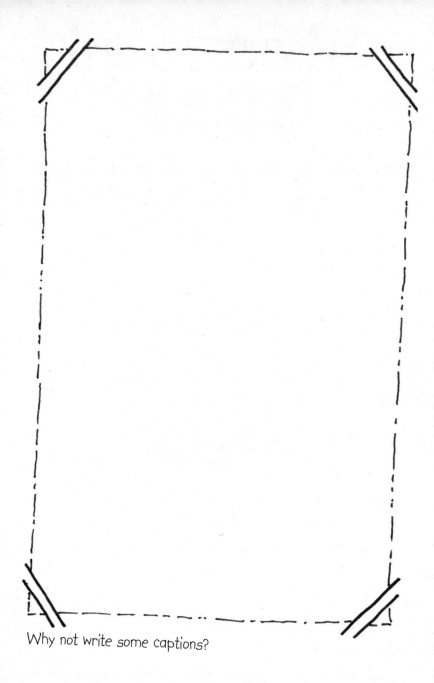

Why not write some captions?

Time to go home!

Every adventure comes to an end.
Now it's time to put out the fire,
pack up and head for home . . .

Put out the fire!
Use a blue pen/crayon
as your 'water'.

Where would you like to go on
your NEXT outdoor adventure?

. . . .

. . . .

. . . .

Like outdoor adventures? Why not join the Scouts?
Find out how at www.scouts.org.uk/join